BRITAIN IN OLD P

QUARRY BANK

NED WILLIAMS
AND MEMBERS OF THE MOUNT PLEASANT
LOCAL HISTORY GROUP

Olive Allchurch, Ivy Astley, Oswald Biddle, Marie Billingham, Mary Brookes,
Doreen Cartwright, Bessie Cranton, Gladys Davies, Bram & Vera Dunn, Horace Dunn,
Jane Geddes, Emma & Ron Hanglin, John James, Patricia Mattocks, Sister Janice Mills,
Joan & Arthur Pearson, Doris Peat, Margaret Priest, Charmayne Redding,
John Robinson, Pauline Rollason, John Shaw, Pat & Sylvia Shaw, Roy Smith,
Frank Whiley and Jessie Yorke.

SUTTON PUBLISHING LIMITED

Sutton Publishing Limited
Phoenix Mill · Thrupp · Stroud
Gloucestershire · GL5 2BU

First published 1998

Front cover : Lower High Street, Quarry Bank
at the beginning of the twentieth century
(see page 23).
Frontispiece: Members of the Local History
Group display the Sunday School banner at
Christ Church.
Back cover: Tourists and visitors to Quarry Bank
were able to buy this five-panel card of local
views until very recent times.

British Library Cataloguing in Publication Data
A catalogue record for this book is available from the
British Library.

ISBN 0-7509-1988-4

Typeset in 10/12 Perpetua.
Typesetting and origination by
Sutton Publishing Limited.
Printed in Great Britain by
Ebenezer Baylis, Worcester

THE BLACK COUNTRY SOCIETY

This voluntary society, affiliated to the Civic Trust, was founded in
1967 as a reaction to the trend of the late 1950s and early 1960s to
amalgamate everything into large units and in the Midlands to
sweep away the area's industrial heritage in the process.

The general aim of the Society is to create interest in the past, present and future of the
Black Country, and early on it campaigned for the establishment of an industrial museum.
In 1975 the Black Country Living Museum was started by Dudley Borough Council on
26 acres of totally derelict land adjoining the grounds of Dudley Castle. This has
developed into an award-winning museum which attracts over 250,000 visitors annually.

It was announced in August 1998 that having secured a lottery grant of nearly £3
million, the Museum Board will be able to authorize the start of work on a £4.5 million
state-of-the-art interpretation centre. This will be known as the 'Rolfe Street Project',
named after the street which once housed the Smethwick Baths. The façade of this
Victorian building is to be incorporated into the new interpretation centre.

At the Black Country Living Museum there is a boat dock fully equipped to restore
narrowboats of wood and iron and different vessels can be seen on the dock throughout
the year. From behind the Bottle and Glass Inn visitors can travel on a canal boat into
Dudley Canal Tunnel, a memorable journey to see spectacular limestone caverns and the
fascinating Castle Mill Basin.

There are 2,500 members of the Black Country Society and all receive the quarterly
magazine *The Blackcountryman*, of which 124 issues have been published since its
founding in 1967. In the whole collection there are some 1,800 authoritative articles on
all aspects of the Black Country by historians, teachers, researchers, students, subject
experts and ordinary folk with an extraordinary story to tell. The whole constitutes a
unique resource about the area and is a mine of information for students and researchers
who frequently refer to it. Many schools and libraries are subscribers. Three thousand
copies of the magazine are printed each quarter. It is non–commercial, and contributors
do not receive payment for their articles.

PO Box 71 · Kingswinford · West Midlands DY6 9YN

CONTENTS

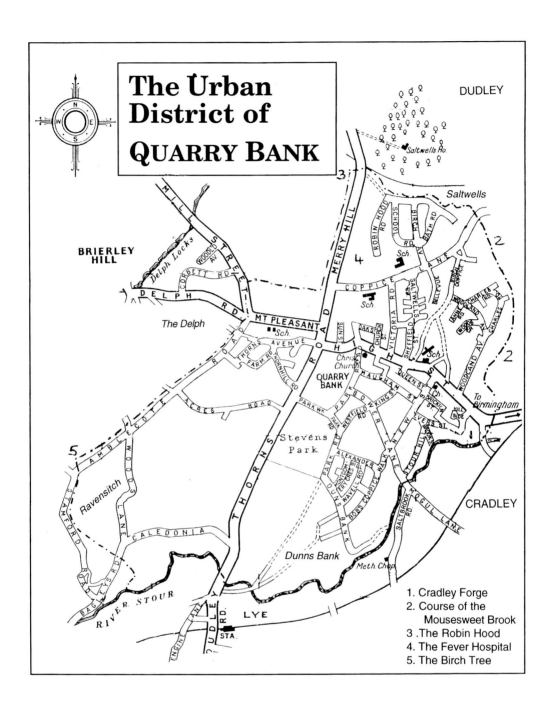

The Urban District of QUARRY BANK

DUDLEY

Saltwells Ro.

Saltwells

BRIERLEY HILL

Delph Locks

The Delph

MT PLEASANT

QUARRY BANK

Stevens Park

Ravensitch

Dunns Bank

CRADLEY

Meth Chap

RIVER STOUR

LYE

STA.

1. Cradley Forge
2. Course of the Mousesweet Brook
3. The Robin Hood
4. The Fever Hospital
5. The Birch Tree

INTRODUCTION

The dim and distant past of Quarry Bank is part of the larger story of Pensnett Chase and the ancient Manor of Kingswinford. Much of the area we now know as Quarry Bank was wooded and human settlement in the area was on a small scale and scattered. Even so, the area had some importance as a route centre on both north to south and east to west axes, and as a frontier between one manor and another. The river Stour was an important natural boundary – first between the manors of Kingswinford and Cradley, later between counties, and of course it still forms the southern boundary of Quarry Bank.

Out west of Quarry Bank, tracks from Amblecote and from Stambermill joined one another near the point where Stamford Road now joins the Amblecote Road, and the track made its way along the top of the bank towards Mount Pleasant. This dramatic ridge, sloping down to The Delph on one side and down to the Stour on the other, brought the traveller by way of Mount Pleasant to the staggered crossroads near Merry Hill. Here the north–south route from Dudley to the Lye crosses the 'bonk' and the west–east route itself descends the bank, down what is now the High Street, and then swings towards Cradley – not towards Cradley Heath as the modern road system does. (A short cut to Cradley could be taken by following Bower Lane.)

Human settlements developed in the clearings in the woods and along these tracks, but there was no growth into anything remotely resembling a town until comparatively recent times. Coal and fireclay was abundantly available beneath the surface throughout the area, but local industry remained very much on a 'cottage' scale. However, the population began to grow as a result of the industrialization of the surrounding areas.

The fact that the population was growing, and that a community of some sort was in the making, was acknowledged by the Church of England. The parish of Kingswinford went through several waves of reorganisation in the first half of the nineteenth century, and Quarry Bank became a distinct parish with its own church in 1845. Methodism by that time was already established in the area and was equally aware of needs of embryonic communities.

Although the first steps towards becoming a modern urban community in the nineteenth century could not have been taken if no one was prosperous, it seems that the majority enjoyed little wealth. Most people in the Quarry Bank area seemed to be associated with poor, or even dying, economic activity like small-scale mining or nail-making. Chain-making perhaps brought a little prosperity, but also seemed to go into a long decline with the advent of more modern chain-making processes. Hand-made chain survived to serve a particular market, but few chain-makers grew rich as a result.

Poverty, and a certain degree of isolation, held Quarry Bank back while surrounding communities became more town-like. Geography isolated Quarry Bank from the canal system and the railway system – such infrastructure tended to put Quarry Bank's neighbours on the map. Similarly, in the twentieth century the Black Country tramway network failed to reach Quarry Bank.

By the second half of the nineteenth century local government was being organised on modern lines. Public bodies were established to consider the needs of local people with regard to matters like roads, health and education. In 1888 Staffordshire County Council was established, and six years later much more localised administrative units had to be established to govern urban and rural districts. Quarry Bank Urban District Council came into being in 1894.

Quarry Bank UDC was small even compared with its neighbour Brierley Hill, but autonomy of a sort encouraged local pride and matched the growing sense of local identity. After all, the establishment of these units of local government meant that someone had to sit down and draw boundaries. The boundary of Quarry Bank UDC still provides a very satisfactory definition of Quarry Bank, even though the Urban District lost its independence in 1934 in becoming part of an enlarged Brierley Hill.

The period 1894–1934 was an exciting one, particularly in the years from 1900 to 1914. It was a period of dramatic change and rapid expansion of the housing environment. Drainage and sewage disposal, street lighting, road-surfacing, public and private building activity, all changed the face of Quarry Bank – as elsewhere. Modern factories (particularly in the hollow-ware trade), new schools and a modern approach to retailing, all helped to create the Quarry Bank that we can glimpse in the earliest photographs used to illustrate this book. The Edwardian era was the heyday of the postcard and popular interest in photography, and this is where a pictorial history of a town like Quarry Bank has to begin.

The early twentieth-century Quarry Bank was still a rather scattered collection of even smaller communities. It is only really the spread of private housing over the last sixty years that has joined such places together. The basic 'crossroad' structure of Quarry Bank still isolates each quadrant thus created, and one of the qualities of Quarry Bank is its maze-like exploitation of the cul-du-sac. The 'dead end' is an urban art form in Quarry Bank – designed to baffle the motorist, but 'interesting' to those who still relate to towns by being a pedestrian. The pedestrian discovers that no apparent dead end is really a dead end. The passage and the track are alive and well in Quarry Bank.

The hollow-ware industry became a major source of employment to the folks of Quarry Bank, but it has to be admitted that the town has possibly been more successful as a place to live than as a place to work. Many Quarry Bankers in the twentieth century must have left their little town in search of work – to the steelworks of Brierley Hill, to the motor industry at Longbridge, and now to the strange retailing phenomenon on Quarry Bank's doorstep: the Merry Hill Centre. Ironically the image of what 'work' meant in Quarry Bank was frozen around the remarkable survival of small-scale chain-making into very recent times, and even the extraction of coal enjoyed a revival in the 1970s.

If Quarry Bank has been a dormitory rather than a workplace, we must be careful not to take the present-day spread of domestic housing to be an accurate reflection of what Quarry Bank has been like. From Victorian times to the 1950s, its isolation was reflected in the way the town seemed surrounded by woods, fields and farmland. This is still reflected in local place names and street names.

To suggest that Quarry Bank owes its distinct individuality to its smallness, its remoteness, or even its place in the socio-economic league table of towns, is to ignore that it has been a very self-sufficient town – quite able to provide everything that a town needs from a cinema to a football team, from drama societies to drinking dens. Thus it is that a book like this is full of pictures of pubs, parks, carnivals, church parades and sporting activities, with Quarry Bankers doing everything imaginable.

Quarry Bank is now part of the large Metropolitan Borough of Dudley, but playing with boundaries has not altered its clear sense of identity as part of what we call the Black Country. The surest way to understand Quarry Bank is to try and understand its part in that unique regional concept: the Black Country – the land where abstract concept and real geography collide to create unique townships with a shared regional identity.

CHAPTER ONE

THE FACE OF QUARRY BANK

The following pages look at the changing face of Quarry Bank. We begin our survey in the High Street, but start the comprehensive tour on page 9 at the crossroads at the centre of the town. From this point we follow the High Street down into the valley of the river Stour, but then return to the crossroads to set off in three other directions. Firstly down Merry Hill towards Coppice Lane, then into Mount Pleasant, and finally down Thorns Road.

We then take in views of the roads that formed the High Street's hinterland: Victoria Road on one side, and then New Street on the other. New Street takes us out to Maughan Street and King Street. A quick glance at Stevens Park follows, then we look at some of the isolated outposts of Quarry Bank including the agricultural frontiers that once separated it so clearly from its neighbours.

Pictures taken in the late 1970s and even the early 1980s show that the late Victorian and early Edwardian heart of Quarry Bank survived, but has been so 'infilled' with later developments that it appears to have changed. The vast expanses of housing built around this heart threaten to swallow up the original township – creating a kind of suburbia that almost obscures the real Quarry Bank.

The High Street has been the centre of Quarry Bank in many different ways: the focus of its urban development, its commercial heart, even a visible reminder of what it means to be on the 'bank', and socially it has been the obvious place to display civic pride in parades and carnivals. Parades by Sunday schools, friendly societies, and coronation celebrations, have all brought Quarry Bankers and photographers to the High Street. This picture by E. Beech shows the Christ Church Sunday School Parade of 1913 heading towards the church. (Frank Webb)

This picture probably shows the New Street Primitive Methodists coming down the High Street in 1908. Note the trees outside the parish church on the left, the lad in Blue-Coat School uniform on the right, and the man with the bowler hat on the left (Henry Bird). Compare this scene with the pictures on pages 13 and 14. (*Julie Dunn*)

The parade that took place on the second day of festivities organised to celebrate the coronation of King George V (23 June 1911) faced a damp start, but involved all Quarry Bank's schoolchildren who were treated to refreshments at school after street parades, followed by sports and games at Mr Barnes' field, and a firework display at Merry Hill. Evans' shop on the left is advertising papers with all the latest news of the coronation. (*Frank Webb*)

The Blue Ball, and the staggered crossroads in front of it, are also candidates for the title of 'centre of Quarry Bank'. Here the old pub is being demolished to make way for its 1960s replacement, while the first step is also taken in the process of widening the road at this junction. (*via Janice Mills*)

A 1950s postcard view of the junction next to the Blue Ball. (The rear extension of the old pub is seen on the extreme left.) The area on the right of the High Street is a Garden of Memory in front of a Sons of Rest building – long since gone! No sign of any traffic, but a passenger stands hopefully at the Midland Red bus stop, and new concrete lamp posts are a sign of post-war modernity. (*Ken Rock*)

This picture of the top of the High Street in Edwardian times complements the previous photograph – the same buildings and walls can be seen in each picture. Frank Webb Snr is standing on the right of the picture in front of Ivy Cottage, a few yards from his mother. (*Frank Webb*)

Frank and Arthur Webb's mother, who lived from 1821 to 1913, stands in the doorway of Ivy Cottage at the top of the High Street – possibly Quarry Bank's oldest surviving buildings. Arthur Webb's yard was behind these cottages, reached from Sun Street. In 1926 Arthur's son, Frank, modernised these cottages, in which form they survive today. In about 1930, Frank Webb built his own house, Hillcroft, opposite Ivy Cottage. Hillcroft also survives today. (*Frank Webb*)

Looking back up the High Street towards the old Sun Inn (replaced in the 1930s), this Edwardian view shows Hawkeswood's ironmongers shop and the High Buildings, also known as Bird's Buildings, which were back-to-back tenements. These photographs were taken by Walter Wootton, Quarry Bank's own photographer with premises at 1 Merry Hill. (*Frank Webb*)

The wall on the right of the above picture enters the left of this picture as we look towards the Royal Oak. The building on the right, on the corner of what was then Bower Lane, now Park Road, must have been demolished soon after this Edwardian photograph was taken. (*Frank Webb*)

The demolition of the High Buildings on the bend of upper High Street in December 1967. On the right is Hawkeswood's ironmongers shop – note the petrol and oil pumps outside. This was probably the site of Quarry Bank's first petrol pump. (*John James*)

With the demolition of the High Buildings, a car park was created on the corner of Park Road and Upper High Street, but this scene has altered yet again in 1998 with the new road access being provided to the High Street. Hawkeswood's shop still stands in 1998 as Jantino brideswear shop. (*Dave Whyley*)

This picture of the north side of the High Street from Oak Street to Church Street, with Cartwright's shop on the right, helps us make our way down the High Street with the church on the opposite side of the road. The Conservative Club is in the centre of the picture, and one or two of the buildings behind the children have been demolished to provide a car park and new access to the club. (*Brenda Holloway*)

A 1970s view of the Royal Oak and the buildings at the top of the High Street as seen from Park Road. In the yard behind the Royal Oak, reached from Oak Street, Pat Collins opened a few fairground attractions each autumn before the First World War. Although the Royal Oak has gone, the new buildings built next door to the site seem to follow this roof pattern. (*Dave Whyley*)

This 1970s view of the High Street shows the bend in the road quite clearly with Salisbury House (of 1892) forming a backdrop. This was demolished in 1998 and the concrete bus shelters have been long gone. Robinson's bakery shops were taken over by Firkins in February 1982. (*John James*)

A close-up of the shop in the background of the picture above will remind readers of The Bike Shop (Homer's) and Mrs Cox's that were on the corner of Oak Street for many years (and double glazing and Indian take-aways by the time of demolition). (*Dave Whyley*)

An E. Beech postcard view of the level stretch of the High Street beyond the Royal Oak in about 1910 – before the road was sealed. (*Frank Webb*)

The Church Tavern, owned by Ansell's, and Sally Wasdell's pharmacy, at the end of the 1970s, by which time Church Street and Oak Street had become a one-way system. (*Dave Whyley*)

This mid-1950s picture evokes the once calm atmosphere of the High Street. Sally Wasdell's pharmacy, on the left, has not yet been extended into the shop next door (Wootton's shoe shop) as in the picture on the previous page. Stringer's little van is parked outside his radio shop, and just beyond the van it is possible to see the road sign warning motorists that they are about to descend the 'bonk' at 1 in 13. (*Bill Bawden*)

A return to the 1970s reminds us of what Dr Rigler's Cottage Surgery looked like when it was two shops: Albert Stringer's radio shop and Rock's fruit and veg shop (V.E. and C.E. Hill). Bennett's shop, the newsagent, had been two shops (Flo Batham's clothes shop and Mrs. Brown's sweets); since then it has become the post office. (*Dave Whyley*)

On the other side of the High Street stands the public library – the brand new building was opened in February 1939, but a branch library had been operating in Quarry Bank since 1936 in temporary premises. In the distance, is the old post office. A pedestrian crossing takes advantage of this straight and level stretch of the High Street in the 1990s. (*Dave Whyley*)

The Co-op stood on the corner of Chapel Street, once known as Z Street because of its shape. The ideals surrounding 'Co-operation' had been presented to Quarry Bankers by the Dudley Co-operative Society during a wave of expansion by that society at the beginning of the 1890s. Records do not reveal whether a Co-op store always existed in Quarry Bank from that time, but the store in this form did not survive the 1980s. (*Dave Whyley*)

As the road begins to descend, Kendall's shops were a feature of the northern 'sunny' side of the High Street – next door to the Dental Laboratory that had once been The Vine public house. The straightforward Victorian design of these shopfronts was still unspoilt in the 1970s. (*Dave Whyley*)

The parade of shops from Victoria Street down to the butcher's shop covers the transition from Upper High Street to Lower High Street. A Jewess' shop had once been Grove's butchers shop. (*Dave Whyley*)

From the end of Sheffield Street the shops on the southern side of the High Street, the 'shady side', are very clearly stepped on this 1 in 13 grade. Freddie Field was once to be found at Central Hairdressing, and Malcolm Bennett's has now become a pet shop. The premises in between had once been Glaze's shop (see page 20). (*Dave Whyley*)

Looking down the 'bonk' from the point where Sheffield Street joins the High Street one can gain a very strong impression of the road descending into the Stour valley, with Cradley in the distance. Before the First World War this was also the point where one passed from Conservative Quarry Bank to Liberal Quarry Bank. (*Dave Whyley*)

Genner's Fish Shop (photographed in the mid-1950s) forms the fish and chip shop in the centre of this row just below Sheffield Street, seen opposite in a slightly later form as The Fryery. Today the two shops in the photo have been amalgamated to make a grander fish and chip shop. (*Gwen Chapman*)

The small shops on the other side of the High Street as the bank steepens seem to have been converted from domestic premises. In such a shop are Mr and Mrs Glaze, their daughters and grandson (Ken Tipton), in the late 1920s. (Mrs Glaze can be seen again on page 92.) (*Ken Tipton*)

On the climb to Sheffield Street, this 1970s picture shows that Genner's fish and chip shop had become The Fryery. Behind these buildings was the yard and garage for Genner's transport fleet. (*Dave Whyley*)

The caretaker's lodge is a little architectural gem in this section of the High Street. Behind it is the end gable of Genner's garage, on which the lettering 'Sunridge Coaches' can still be seen – faintly. This fleet name was only used for a brief period (see page 91). (*Ned Williams*)

One of Kendall's postcards of Quarry Bank in the early 1930s shows the lodge and the school buildings that were demolished in about 1937, after new schools had opened. (*Judith Simpson*)

An earlier view, from a John Price postcard, looking up the High Street, once again shows the school buildings that extended the original Board School of 1872 on the right of the picture. When the surface of the road became rutted in wet weather, the 'sludge' was pushed to one side, taken away, dried out and then reapplied to the surface of the road and compressed. This endless cycle continued until the roads were sealed with tarmac. (*Frank Webb*)

This E. Beech postcard of Lower High Street is more elegant than the John Price version and shows the buildings on the left-hand side of the street more clearly. Dunn's Bakery cart is seen behind the well-dressed boys. Among the buildings on the left was the practice of Dr Francis Maylett Smith who has written about his life (1916 to 1933) in Quarry Bank in *A G.P.'s Progress to the Black Country*. (*Frank Webb*)

Another important building in this part of the High Street is the Liberal Club. Mrs Bills, the stewardess, gazes from the window in this view. In the evening of 19 December 1940 a German parachute mine landed in this building but did not explode. The heroic struggle to defuse it safely was the work of several Quarry Bankers, including Frank Webb. The fact that such bombs fell on Quarry Bank but caused so little destruction earned the town the nickname 'The Holy City'. (*Horace Dunn*)

Lower High Street begins to level out a little beyond the schools and the Labour Club car park looks out on these buildings, all of which have undergone changes since this picture was taken at the end of the 1970s. On the far right is the Queen's Head. (*Dave Whyley*)

The Queen's Head, already closed, forms the left-hand side of this picture as we look down Lower High Street towards the Mobil service station that stood for a time on the site of the Coronet cinema. (*Dave Whyley*)

Next to the Queen's Head was Shaw Brothers, builders, painters and decorators, and J.G. Motors, which grew into QB Bikes and moved further down the road. (*Dave Whyley*)

pposite the Mobil service station was The Three Horseshoes – another of Quarry Bank's vanished pubs. The houses on e right are representative of the solid homes built during the last quarter of the nineteenth century as Quarry Bank went rough rapid urbanisation. The High Street dips towards Cradley Forge and leaves the town. (*Dave Whyley*)

Before leaving the world of the High Street we look at the Victorian houses that stretched into the hinterland of the High Street, as illustrated in this glimpse of Chapel Street – known for years as Z Street. Queen Street and Maughan Street also extended Quarry Bank's 'brick environment' into the triangle between the High Street, New Street and Bower Lane, just as Victoria Road and Sheffield Street extended the town towards Coppice Lane. (*Dave Whyley*)

The houses in Rose Hill seem to date from an even earlier period. It is still an interesting road to explore, with a smallholding surviving on the right, and a footpath leading from the end of Rose Hill out on to the coal tips of Saltwells No. 33 Colliery, which closed in about 1912! (*Dave Whyley*)

To continue our exploration of Quarry Bank we return to the crossroads at the top of the High Street, and look down Merry Hill from the corner of Mount Pleasant. Walter Wootton took the picture and was perhaps impressed with the modernity of the new gas lamp, *c.* 1908. The shop on the corner was demolished and the corner occupied by Hanke's coalyard for many years. (*Robert Chell*)

The view up Merry Hill, towards the crossroads, from just below the junction with Coppice Lane: the photographer must be standing at the point where Quarry Bank's northern boundary heads west along Two Woods Lane. Coal was extracted from the area to the right, but eventually houses were built all the way up to Mount Pleasant. (*Ken Rock*)

Twenty years ago the Coppice Lane roundabout was an obvious frontier to Quarry Bank, and the view beyond looked out across pastures, where once coal had been extracted, towards the Round Oak Steel Works at Brierley Hill. Recently some shops have been built in this no-man's land between Quarry Bank and Brierley Hill. (*Dave Whyley*)

This elegant turn-of-the-century house still stands on the corner of Coppice Lane and Victoria Road. (Most other 'roads' in Quarry Bank were 'streets'.) Its original position on the frontier of Quarry Bank can be understood by studying the skyline in the lower picture on page 82. (*Frank Webb*)

An E. Beech postcard of Mount Pleasant in about 1910 looking towards the Amblecote Road. On the right is The Brickmaker public house, and further away, on the left, it is possible to make out the steeple above the entrance to Mount Pleasant School peeping above the roof of the Infants Department. Magnification of the original card reveals that the bread cart comes from The Home Bakery (Dunn's) opposite the school. (*Frank Webb*)

Mount Pleasant looking from the Amblecote Road end back towards town. This charming Edwardian view shows the Wesleyan Chapel before its front was altered with a new extension (see page 58), and the four houses that separated the chapel from Mount Pleasant School. The first building we can see belonging to the school is the new workshop built in 1912 to house woodwork and domestic science classrooms. (*Ken Rock*)

In Quarry Bank shops are used as landmarks as often as pubs. It seems that you knew you were in Mount Pleasant once you had passed Freda Price's. Here is Freda herself standing in the doorway of her newly acquired premises. She was to be found in this shop for forty years. (*Vicky Horton*)

Freda's shop can be seen at the right-hand end of the block that ran round the corner from Thorn's Road into Mount Pleasant. (Freda's own name now adorns the shop.) The door on the corner led into 'Aunty's', with her café on the left and her cake shop on the right. (*John James*)

The buildings illustrated opposite contained more shops as they made their way towards Thorns Road, opposite the Blue Ball. On the left was Walter Wootton's photography shop at 1 Merry Hill. To the right of the entry were two other shops run by the Woottons, selling millinery and haberdashery; on the extreme right was Allport's fish shop. This picture was taken in the mid-1960s. (*John James*)

Some fine houses were built on several sections of Thorns Road in Victorian times, but other sections of Thorns Road seemed to pass 'open country' until a much later period. Young Doris Sidaway stands at the gate of 81 Thorns Road in the mid-1930s. The family's house, behind her, was demolished in the 1930s when replaced with a new house built behind it. (*Doris Peat*)

Kendall's two postcard views of Thorns Road show how the road developed. This view shows some of the Victorian villa that eventually found themselves looking out over the park. The house on the right is no. 66, and the tree towards the le has replaced a monkey puzzle tree. (*Judith Simpson*)

The second study of Thorns Road, taken further down towards The Lye, opposite the lower end of the park, shows so of the inter-war housing that filled in the gaps between the older houses. The house on the left is no. 136. (*Judith Simps*

Quarry Bank's first wave of expansion in late Victorian times is illustrated in this view of Victoria Road. Arthur Webb's building company had been founded in 1887, and built a few houses on each side of Victoria Road at the High Street end. This picture was taken from the Coppice Lane end of the road. The cemetery was established by the church in 1900 and looks very new – young trees and fresh gravestones. (*Frank Webb*)

Kendall's postcard view of the cemetery was taken a few years later when the trees had begun to grow, and also shows the small chapel built there in 1903 – of which no trace now remains. Coppice Lane climbs across the back of this view, and the Boys Secondary School was built on the high ground obscured by the chapel. (*Judith Simpson*)

New Street was an important thoroughfare by the end of the last century, with its Victorian houses, Primitive Methodist Chapel, and generous supply of shops. This picture, by E. Beech, shows the chapel effectively and one of the shops of Edwin Cox, a chemist. The poster in his doorway advertises the Palace cinema at the Lye, better known as 'The Temp', and the hoardings advertise LNWR excursions to Rhyl. (*Frank Webb*)

An excellent picture of Joe Goodwin's store in New Street. Joe is second from the left, and his son, John Goodwin, fourth from the left. Joe Goodwin opened the shop in 1875, and it was eventually run by John until his retirement, having been open for a century! (*Pat Mattocks*)

'Severed last night' has been written on the back of this picture of Goodwin's shop in New Street during the aftermath of the Quarry Bank Food Riots – events that were sparked off by food shortages towards the end of the First World War. Shopkeepers were unpopular as a result of rationing, if they were suspected of selling goods at more than the 'controlled' price, or if they happened to serve on the Food Committees that were set up to deal with the shortages. (*Marie Billingham*)

Next door to Goodwin's, on the approach to the corner of Maughan Street, was the 'oil shop', where everyone has paused in their work to pose for the camera. Both Goodwin's, and the remains of this shop, are now derelict. (*via Janice Mills*)

Maughan Street looking down towards New Street, *c.* 1910. On the right is a public house, The Cottage in the Bower, and in the distance, on the far side of the Stour vale, is Cradley. (*Frank Webb*)

This picture of King Street tells the same story of Quarry Bank's piecemeal Victorian development – leaving open space to be 'infilled' later. The Sunday School parade is making its way towards Bower Lane, some time before the First World War. It is tempting to believe that the banner at the front of the procession – almost in Bower Lane – is the same banner that is shown on page 1. (*Frank Webb*)

No survey of Quarry Bank would be complete without some views of Stevens Park. Immediately after the First World War, Ernest Stevens gave this stretch of land, in two separate gifts, to the people of Quarry Bank. As in other Black Country towns such open space, destabilised by coal working, could only be landscaped and turned into a public park. In this picture Quarry Bank UDC formerly accepts the gift and Ernest Stevens declares the park open on 16 July 1921. (*Jack Beddall*)

The money to build a bandstand in Stevens Park was donated to Quarry Bank by Ernest and Mary Stevens in March 1925, not long before Mary's death. Ernest opened it in her memory on 22 August 1925. The Quarry Bank Silver Band, directed by Mr T.H. Bloomer, joined Ernest Stevens on the bandstand to inaugurate it, and played again from the bandstand that evening.

Ernest Stevens not only gave the land to the people of Quarry Bank for a park, he also contributed to the fund established to turn it into a park and provided the bandstand, 150 tons of sand for the children's sand heap, and this paddling pool. The three boys by the pool are Victor Stevens, and brothers Harry and Frank Billingham. (*Jessie Yorke*)

The war memorial was erected as a result of public subscriptions; it was inspired by the design of London's Cenotaph and is a major feature of the park. Steps towards erecting the memorial were not taken until 1925 – after most surrounding towns – but the Council had put a memorial in the church. Arthur Taylor (see page 122) is among the familiar Quarry Bank surnames appearing on the memorial. The smaller monument to the right lists the men who died during the Second World War. (*Ned Williams*)

We conclude our tour of Quarry Bank with glimpses of some of the outermost reaches of the township. The road in the foreground and the brine baths to the right are in Quarry Bank. The Mousesweet Brook flows just behind the baths and everything beyond it, including the Saltwells Inn, is in the Netherton ward of Dudley. Saltwells never grew into a prosperous spa, but it was still possible to bathe in its very saline water up until the 1930s. (*Ken Rock*)

The Isolation Hospital, or 'Fever Hospital', was deliberately remote from the rest of Quarry Bank. It was approached by a track from the Pedmore Road and was hidden from view by Merry Hill – it is now under Robin Hood Road. Mr and Mrs Beddall are seen here, in about 1910, in their capacity as caretakers of the building. For readers interested in the construction of pre-fabricated corrugated-iron fever hospitals – one survives today as the village hall at Wolverley! (*Doris Peat*)

Merry Hill Farm was still worked by Mr Thomas in the 1950s, and this field looked out across the basin where coal had been extracted and where the land had partly returned to pasture and was partly derelict. Round Oak Steel Works dominates the skyline. Farms and steelworks have gone: the Merry Hill Centre has arrived. (*Bill Bawden*)

Ravensitch Farm still exists, and has been in the hands of the Wright family for three generations. It is on the south-facing slope of the Amblecote bank, in an area in which farms once had to co-exist with fireclay workings and shallow coal pits, but which is now dominated by housing. (*Ned Williams*)

CHAPTER TWO

THE CHURCHES

During the early nineteenth century the village of Quarry Bank was part of the large parish of Kingswinford, centred from 1831 onwards at Holy Trinity Church, Wordsley. In 1844 the Privy Council recommended to Queen Victoria that the parish be divided into new smaller parishes in line with the ideas expressed by Robert Peel's Royal Commission. The Anglican Church was trying to modernise, and to catch up with the non-conformists in reaching the souls of the rapidly expanding industrial areas of Britain.

Thus on 3 September 1844, the Revd W. Cox found himself appointed the first minister of this new parish. An old nail warehouse in Vine Street (now Victoria Road) had been purchased and was used for services until a 'proper' church could be built. This building was also used as a National School during weekdays, and was later used as a Sunday School. It was drastically rebuilt in 1913 to continue as a Sunday School and Church Hall until 1997.

Quarry Bank's new parish church was built on the corner of Bower Lane and the High Street on land that had belonged to a Joseph Stevens. The foundation stone was laid by Amelia, Baroness Ward, on 28 October 1845 and the church was built in seventeen months. It was consecrated on 2 March 1847.

In its 150-year history Christ Church has gone through many changes, modernisations and alterations – including recovery from a fire which occurred on 19 November 1900. Its dramatic location and striking visual appearance give it an enviable prominence in Quarry Bank. The yellow bricks with which it is constructed are a symbolic gift from local industry: the mining of fireclay and the manufacture of refractory bricks. Without moving a single brick, the church was transferred from the Diocese of Lichfield to the Diocese of Worcester in October 1993.

Methodist missionaries came to the area in the 1820s, and their first chapel in Quarry Bank opened in 1830 in Sheffield Street. A 'new' chapel of 1845, built in the Rose Hill area lasted until 1860. The land in New Street appears to have been purchased in about 1850, but it was not until 1860 that the chapel was completed on that site. Its replacement was enlarged in 1873 but was then destroyed by mining subsidence in 1897. The final New Street Chapel opened in 1903 and survived until 1981.

Birch Coppice Methodist Church appears to have started life in 1884 in a small wooden building, under the wing of the New Street church. In 1888 Birch Coppice gained a brand new 'tin church' seating 300 people.

The corrugated-iron church was a great success and was soon bursting at the seams. Many years passed while trying to raise enough money to build a replacement, until efforts were rewarded by construction work commencing in 1957. The new Sunday School was opened in March 1958, the tin chapel was demolished and the new brick-built church was opened in August 1958. A Hammond organ was provided in 1964.

John Wesley is supposed to have visited the district in 1770 and the Wesleyan Methodists were soon established in the area. The congregations met in houses until chapels could be built. Land in Mount Pleasant was acquired in July 1828 for such a purpose and a foundation stone was laid within a few days of the purchase. By the end of November of that year the chapel was opened. A school was built the following year, and was subsequently rebuilt on two occasions. The church, like others in the area, had its share of worries when it came to local mine workings, buying some mineral rights in 1839 to safeguard the building, and buying the remainder from the Earl of Dudley in 1907.

Up until 1925 the church had a fairly plain Georgian brick frontage, and an unadorned interior, but all this was changed in a rebuild made financially possible by Ernest Stevens – and the modernised chapel was reopened on 22 June 1927.

At the other end of Quarry Bank, the Methodists claim an ancestry going back to a society that existed during the time of John Wesley's visit, although at the time the congregation met in Cradley. In 1796 this small congregation appears to have moved into Quarry Bank by purchasing a chapel at Cradley Forge, probably on the Wagon & Horses side of the road.

Later the Cradley Forge Methodists had become part of the New Connexion when the Methodists divided in 1835. They crossed the road in 1850 to begin using a new chapel built at the foot of Hammer Bank. This building lasted until July 1938 and was demolished when the road was widened. Ten years earlier the congregation had built a new Sunday School building at the top of Hammer Bank and this became the church itself from 1938 onwards. A Hammond organ was installed in the church in September 1939.

The 1835 division of the Methodist Church had also affected the Wesleyans at Mount Pleasant, and eight of the eleven original trustees had left the church in that year. It seems that some of them may have established a New Connexion chapel in Talbots Lane, later known as the Bethany Chapel. Those who can remember this building recall a large plain brick Georgian-style structure – eventually weakened by mining activity.

Another independently-minded congregation was established in the mid-1880s in a building that had once been a soap factory. 'The Soap Hole' appears to have been close to Merry Hill on the Mount Pleasant side of the road. Perhaps this church grew out of the Temperance Movement of the time: the Blue Ribbon Army.

Somewhere in its history this group joined the Congregational Union, and in 1897 had moved to a mission hall in the quaintly named Z Street (now Chapel Street). During the inter-war period these Congregationalists set out once more to improve their place of worship. The new building, in the High Street, was opened on 6 July 1935 at a cost of over £2,000 – about half of which had been raised by the congregation.

The Z Street Mission was retained as a Sunday School – and there was access to it from the back of the new church. It was demolished in the '60s when the new prefabricated Sunday School building next door to the 1935 church was opened in 1967.

When the Congregationalists joined with the Presbyterians to form the United Reformed Church, the Quarry Bank church decided not to be part of the merger, and has remained an independent church within the Evangelical Fellowship of Congregational Churches. It prides itself on still having a Sunday School and looks back to the times when it had an excellent choir led by Sam Bushell, a chain maker who was choirmaster, bandmaster and church treasurer.

Looking towards the altar at Christ Church Quarry Bank at the beginning of this century. The church interior has been through several periods of alteration since its consecration on 2 March 1847 but most noticeable in this picture are the elaborate pew-ends which are no longer a feature of the church. The east window was provided in memory of a Mrs Billingham who died in 1897. (*Church collection*)

The Kendall's postcard view of Christ Church's interior shows the brass lectern given to the church by Ernest Stevens and the Revd T.J. McNulty's stone pulpit. Looking at the names of the donors of the numerous gifts to the church over the years provides a 'who's who' of Quarry Bankers connected with the church. (*Judith Simpson*)

Left: The Revd T. Carpenter Dixon, second vicar at Christ Church (1854–1893), in which time the first organ was installed, and oil lamps gave way to gas lamps. Mr Dixon had a great deal to do with establishing and running the National School.

Bottom left: The Revd T. J. McNulty, third vicar at Christ Churc, (1893–1920), during a period which first saw the church extended and then badly damaged by fire in 1900. He also added the churchyard and chapel in Victoria Road (1903), and rebuilt the Sunday School building (1913).

Below: The Revd A H. Vizard – an ex-Army chaplain who was vicar at Christ Church from 1920 to 1923. He established the Men's Movement (a revival of an idea first developed by Mr McNulty), delivered wonderful sermons, and set up the Parochial Church Council. (Subsequent vicars are illustrated elsewhere.) (*All three photos from Frank Webb*)

The Young Men's Class, September 1930. Back row, left to right: Alfred Bellfred, Clarence Marchant, Jack Brookes, Bill Thompson, B. Mason, Bernard Allport. Centre row: Ronnie Billingham, Percy Whitehouse, Ben Dunn (The Leader), the Revd W. McCarthy, Leslie Chell, Herbert Dunn, Frank Bills. Front row: Jimmy Little, George Price, Lesley Grainger, Jack Whitehouse. (Herbert Dunn was a son of Ben, and can be seen again on page 88; Jack Whitehouse can be found on page 99.) (*Church collection*)

Christ Church Sunday School teachers on a trip to Blackpool, 1947. (*Marie Billingham*)

Amelia, Baroness Ward laid the foundation stone of the church in October 1845, but its story begins with an Order in Council of 3 September 1844 when the parish of Quarry Bank was created out of the former parish of Kingswinford. This picture was taken on the 150th anniversary of that event and features the churchwardens Jack Hill and Geoffrey Harper, and their wives Mary and Adelaide. It also features the most dramatic view of the church itself – from 'the Bower'. (*Church collection*)

The church Men's Movement was started in 1920, followed by a Women's Movement, reconstituted as the Mothers' Union in 1926. Here we see the Revd G. Larkin (1946–1972), soon after the war, with members of the Men's Movement. Next to him stands Herbert Dunn, leader of the Movement and lay-reader. (*Church collection*)

The Revd George Larkin was a popular and well-known vicar who attended to many parochial issues – including the state of the drains. Sorting out the drains from left to right we can see George Webb, Michael Larkin, Charlie Silcox, George Larkin, W. Brinckler, Syd Homer and Sid Priest. (*Ivy Homer*)

Cleaning up the churchyard in 1973. Left to right: June Grove, Vera White, the Revd Victor Irwin, Willie Irwin, Frank Williams and W. Brinckler. (*June Grove*)

When the Revd Victor Irwin arrived in 1972 he carried on Revd Larkin's care of the church's physical environment as well as its spiritual welfare. A £4,000 restoration was completed in November 1974 – after which the ladies of the church had to clean up. June Grove, Doris Peat and Dora Smith are on the top step; Bessie King, Jeanne Haywood, Tissie Hill and Bessie Cranton are kneeling (*June Grove*)

Aubrey Burrows was church organist at Christ Church when this picture was taken in July 1980. In 1985 he left to become organist at St Peter's, Cradley. The original church organ was installed in the 1860s, delivered via The Delph by canal, and was replaced by a new organ in 1923. (*Church collection*)

The Church choir in 1968 – about the time the choirboys had threatened to strike for better pay! Included among the faces are: front left, Michael White, now a professor in the USA; Nicholas Pearson, now a chartered engineer; and Michael Grove, now a deputy head teacher (see page 11), In the middle towards the right are Maurice Evans, a member of the choir for years, and Harold Burrows. The back row includes Graham Nunn (later head master at Mount Pleasant School, and Aubrey Burrows, church organist. (*Church collection*)

The Church choir, *c.* 1910. The Revd T.J. McNulty can be seen on the left. (*Church collection*)

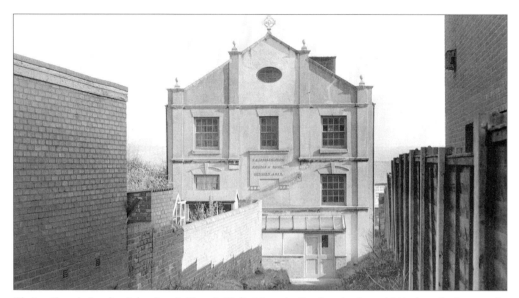

Christ Church Sunday School and Church Hall, Victoria Road, rebuilt in 1913, by which time the eighteenth-century building was in a very poor state. The former nail warehouse had also housed the National School from 1866 for about ten years.

Clergy, churchwardens, Sunday School superintendents and teachers of Christ Church, 1926. Seated in the centre is the Rev. Mr Wood, and next to him is Ben Dunn who has three sons standing in the row behind him: Albert, Herbert (associated with Jury Hollow) and, at the end of the row, Alfred. On the vicar's left is Herbert Grainger, later a Rowley Regis councillor. On the back row in the centre is Joe Warwick, of the local hollow-ware firm, and on the extreme right is Harry Hawkeswood, scoutmaster. This was the period when Quarry Bank's politics were split in three directions – and all factions are represented in this picture! (*Church collection*)

The New Street Primitive Methodist Chapel just before its demolition in 1981. This building was completed in 1901 after its predecessor built on the same site in 1860 was destroyed by subsidence. (*Dave Whyley*)

The interior of the New Street chapel, after the organ had been installed in 1905 at a cost of £375, half of which was paid by the Andrew Carnegie Foundation. The chapel accommodated 500 people. (*Mary Rousell*)

The Wesleyan Methodists of the New Connexion were established at Cradley Forge, where there is some complicated chapel history to sort out. From about 1850 onwards they used a chapel at the foot of Hammer Bank that lasted until 1938. In 1928 they began building a new Sunday School at the top of Hammer Bank, and this, in turn, has become the church. Here they are seen laying the first bricks at Hammer Bank in 1928. (*Tom and Sybil Genner*)

The Cradley Forge Church at the end of Hammer Bank. The footpath in the foreground descends steeply into the River Stour's valley.

In 1948 a plaque was unveiled at Cradley Forge Church in memory of three men who had given many year's service to the church: David Hadlington, Ralph Homer and Henry Homer. Standing, left to right: Ron Capewell, William Jones, Norman Bucknall, the Revd Case, -?-, Horace Grove, Henry Davies. Seated: Mrs Henry Homer, Ralph Homer, Mrs Hadlington. (*Tom and Sybil Genner*)

During the 1920s, the Cradley Forge Sunday School building provided facilities for amateur dramatics that grew out of concerts and religious plays, but soon became a full-blown amateur operatic and dramatic society (see page 100 onwards). In this 1940 production of *Jack & The Beanstalk* we can see many of the stalwarts of the society: Jack Felton and Clarence Tipton as Snip and Snop, Dick Bedford as Squire Hardup and Ernie Webb as Dame Trot, plus Jessie the cow. These shows paid off the mortgage on the building. (*Brenda Holloway*)

The Z Street Mission Hall.

The Congregational Church choir. Sam Bushell, the choirmaster, was a chain-maker by trade, but was also church treasurer and bandmaster. It is believed that the Quarry Bank Silver Band grew out of the Temperance Band established by this congregation, and Sam was part of the band for fifty years. (*Alan Southall*)

The Congregationalists built themselves a new church in the High Street, which opened on 6 July 1935. It was built by A.J. Crump of Dudley to designs of Messrs Gething & Rolley, and cost over £2,000 – half of which had already been raised by the congregation. It replaced the Z Street Mission Hall of 1897, seen on the opposite page, which the Congregationalists had come to from their original home in the old soap works! The church is still independent, not part of the United Reformed Church. (*Alan Southall*)

Crowds flock into the new Sunday School building built next door to the Congregational Church at its opening in 1967. This building finally made the Z Street hall redundant. (*Alan Southall*)

Everyone has their coat on, despite the coke stove in the foreground, in this picture of the Sunday School in progress at the Tin Chapel at Birch Coppice. (*Joy Woodhouse*)

The Tin Chapel at Birch Coppice was brand new in 1888, and replaced an earlier wooden building which then found further use when it moved to Hayes Lane. The congregation seems to have been formed in 1884, under the wing of the New Street Primitive Methodists. Tin chapels are now very rare in the Black Country but examples have been preserved in the museums at Avoncroft (Bromsgrove) and Blists Hill (Ironbridge). This picture was taken in 1958 when the building was about to be demolished. (*Joy Woodhouse*)

The girls at the Sunday School at Birch Coppice Chapel sit down to refreshments some time in 1951–52. Val Cartwright is fourth from the left. (*Roy Smith*)

The new brick chapel at Birch Coppice was opened in August 1958. A Hammond organ was added in 1964. Left to right: Margaret Price, Reg Sidaway, Joy Woodhouse, Mary Flohr, Mary Rousell. (*Joy Woodhouse*)

The Wesleyan Chapel at the end of Mount Pleasant was opened in 1928. In this picture the extended frontage is clearly visible. It was financed by Ernest Stevens and opened in 1927. (The frontage before this was added can be seen on page 29.) Behind the chapel was a school room which went through several rebuilds, ending up with a superb moulded terracotta frontage. It was demolished in the 1980s. (*Ned Williams*)

The building behind the Mount Pleasant chapel was home to Sunday School, Youth Club and so on. On this occasion the Youth Club stand at the back of the picture while entertaining members of the Sunday School, including D'Arcy Jones (fourth from left), Oliver Plant and his wife Clare who had started the club, and Bill Holden who was caretaker at the church at the time. (Pat Mattocks)

CHAPTER THREE

THE PUBS

Quarry Bank is like other Black Country townships in that brewing was widely practised on a domestic basis. The nail shop or chain shop behind your home was often complemented by the brew-house. Public houses also brewed their own beer, and, of course, like any self-respecting town, Quarry Bank eventually had its own brewery. To put things in perspective, Quarry Bank also had its own Temperance supporters.

The pubs of Quarry Bank, like its churches and schools, can be seen as another component of the local topography. What is interesting therefore, is what has survived, what has changed, and what has vanished. Many 'traditional' Black Country pubs of Quarry Bank have vanished, as well as the brewery. Of the survivors, such as The Brickmaker, The White Horse, The New Inn, The Fountain, and the re-named Church Tavern, some have changed more than others.

Pubs of other architectural eras are also to be found in Quarry Bank, ranging from the 1930s 'roadhouse' style of The Roebuck to the 1980s style of the Corn Exchange – already in its second incarnation! Unfortunately no period pictures came to hand of the 1960s pubs that grew up to cope with the residential expansion of Quarry Bank, such as The Birch Coppice, The Thorns and The Caledonia.

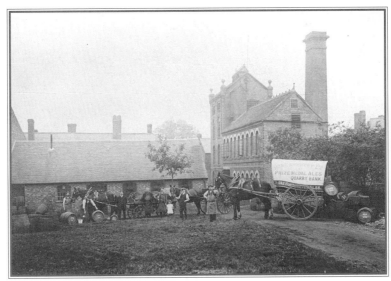

The Home Brewery in Ever Street in 1908, while under the control of Joseph Paskin Simpkiss. J.P. Simpkiss ran the Home Brewery from 1903 until 1916, mainly as a wholesale brewer serving a wide area, but with a few local tied houses. Its subsequent owners ceased brewing in 1921 despite many plans for expansion. The buildings were demolished in 1959. (Jim Webb)

We begin our survey of Quarry Bank's pubs by looking at two that are right on the frontiers of Quarry Bank. The Birch Tree greets travellers making for Quarry Bank via the Amblecote Road. It was still a Simpkiss pub when this picture was taken in the 1970s and the spoil from open-cast coal workings of that time can be seen behind the pub to the right. (It became a Simpkiss pub in the 1930s when J.P. Simpkiss was brewing in Brierley Hill – not from the Home Brewery.) (*Charley Grice*)

The Robin Hood on the Pedmore Road welcomes travellers to Quarry Bank from Dudley. (Technically the pub is a few yards into Brierley Hill.) William Hughes appears to have been the landlord when this turn-of-the-century photograph was taken. In more recent times Ray Hingley popularised Black Country Night Outs at the Robin Hood, and was host to the Citizens' Theatre. (*Jabe Edwards*)

The Royal Oak Hotel commanded a good position at the top of Quarry Bank's High Street, and was selling Atkinsons Aston Ales at the end of the 1920s when this picture was taken of the ox-roast put on to support the carnival. The Quarry Bank Wake had once been held in the yard at the back of the Royal Oak, and further pictures of this pub can be found on page 13. (*Mary Watson*)

The New Inn also occupies a good position on the High Street, and survives today without much alteration. A coach and four stands outside the New Inn in 1935 as part of local celebrations of King George V's jubilee. The licensee was then Henry Stevens. (*Gwen Chapman*)

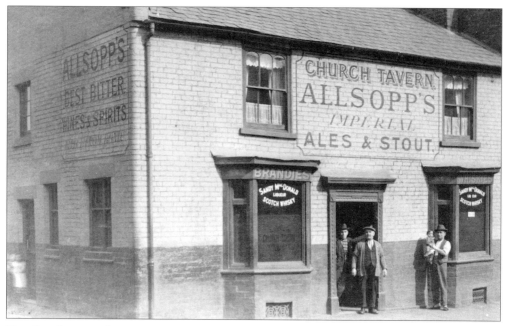

The Church Tavern features in many High Street pictures, and has recently been reincarnated as The Nailmaker. Name changes to landmark pubs can be confusing, and it seems local coach operators still say, 'We'll pick you up at the Church Tavern.' (*Geoff Jones*)

The Vine, on the corner of Victoria Road and the High Street, is now much altered as the Dental Laboratory. It was once the meeting place of Quarry Bank's pigeon fanciers. (*Jack Beddall*)

The Queen's Head looks very forlorn in Lower High Street as it awaits demolition at the beginning of the 1980s. (*Dave Whyley*)

Another vanished pub is the Pilgrim's Cottage, once to be found at Cradley Forge, almost on the bank of the Stour. It was bought by J.P.D. Simpkiss of the Home Brewery in 1914 and was sold again in 1921 when the brewery closed. It was delicensed in 1927. (*Jack Beddall*)

The Fountain Inn still stands proudly in Victoria Road, but its glazed brickwork looks very new in this early 1900s picture by E. Beech. At the time it was an Atkinson's house, licensed by Annie Glaze. In 1906 a murder occurred in a cottage behind The Fountain, bringing a little notoriety to this respectable Quarry Bank street where several Quarry Bank UDC officials lived. It was acquired by Batham's in 1931 and was then sold to William Butler in 1933. (*Frank Webb*)

The Hope & Anchor was quite a substantial public house in Bower Lane, seen here at the beginning of the 1980s. (*Dave Whyley*)

The Cottage in the Bower was to be found at the top of Maughan Street until the 1980s. The engraved glass in the windows carried the legend 'G Nock's Famous Ales'. (*Dave Whyley*)

A room inside the Cottage in the Bower, featuring the timber partitioning found in many Black Country locals. (*Dave Whyley*)

The Brickmaker's Arms is still to be found in Mount Pleasant, where it is popularly known as The Brick. The proprietor, Joe Hollis, brewed his own beer – hence the sign, and there was once a fine bowling green at the back of the pub. (*Olive Allchurch*)

The Vine (or Bull and Bladder) is a few yards from the frontier of Quarry Bank, at the top of The Delph, but the Batham family had associations with Quarry Bank, and various young Bathams attended Mount Pleasant Primary School (including David Batham, 1932–8, and Timothy Arthur Joseph Batham, 1963–9).

CHAPTER FOUR

THE SCHOOLS

The first school in Quarry Bank was the National & Parochial Mixed School, which was opened on 1 January 1866 in premises on the site of the present-day Sunday School building between Victoria Road and Sheffield Street. National Schools were provided by the Church of England in the first step towards providing education for all. The Revd Dixon, his curate, and some of the ladies from the Christ church congregation, were very involved in this first attempt at educating the unruly children of the miners and metal-workers that inhabited the growing township of Quarry Bank. The headmaster, Mr Duffield, assisted by members of his family, often recorded his difficulties in the school log book as he tried to persuade his pupils to attend punctually and regularly, and 'tame' them to accept the rigours and rituals of schooling. Education cost 4d a week, with a discount for more than one child coming from a family.

The Education Act of 1870 established School Boards that had to assess the educational needs of their area and then had to set about building schools to meet those needs. Quarry Bank was in a large area covered by the Kingswinford School Board, and the Board opened its first school in Quarry Bank on 15 July 1872. The headmaster, James Massey, began work with just twenty-four children but numbers improved after some work put in by the Attendance Officer. The school broke up for two weeks in September but when it opened again it boasted seventy pupils, quickly rising to over one hundred. Like the National School, the Board School battled with discipline problems and attendance problems. In July 1874, the Inspector noted, '*I regret that I am unable to report any improvement in this school since my last visit.*'

It is not quite clear what building was being used by the Board School, but it is assumed to be the building that eventually housed the infants, and which still stands in Lower High Street today. The Inspectors regularly complained about the premises and looked forward to the day when bigger premises would be provided. This day seems to have arrived in August 1877 when the new school opened in separate departments with provision for 170 girls, 170 boys and 250 mixed infants. The 'new' premises are assumed to be the school seen in the well-known postcard view of Lower High Street (see page 69). Once the Board School was open in this enlarged form, the National School seems to have closed.

The Inspectors were never very positive about what they found in Quarry Bank – as shown by the comment of 1880: 'I begin my report by saying that the neighbourhood of Quarry Bank is a backward one, and that high results are not to be expected for some years to come. The transition from absolute ignorance to proper education must be very gradual.' This was tough on the schools who were partly paid by results, and on the children of Quarry Bank who had to pay 3d a week for the privilege of wrestling with the educational system.

In September 1882, the School Board opened another school in Quarry Bank – at Mount Pleasant. This school, under Sarah Jane Austen, struggled to make the best of temporary premises in the Sunday School building at the back of Mount Pleasant's Wesleyan Chapel. Once again the Inspectors found adverse things to say about both the pupils and the premises. Matters improved in Mount Pleasant on 10 September 1888 when the new buildings were opened, in which Miss Austen continued to run the Infants Department and the famous Mr Hunt began his forty-two year reign at the helm of the Mixed Juniors.

At Mount Pleasant the school survives in the much rebuilt, extended, and improved School Board buildings. Down in Quarry Bank the Juniors moved into a new building in April 1937 – the boys on the ground floor, and the girls on the floor above. Although the Board School buildings had been well built, the polluted air of the Black Country attacked the Bath stone with which they were constructed – hence the need for new buildings!

The 1930s also saw the proper provision of secondary education arrive in Quarry Bank. On 5 October 1932 the Senior Boys School with Mr. Badger at the helm opened on one side of Coppice Lane, and the Senior Girls School opened with Miss Florence Woolridge on the other side. Neither school was completed at the time and the formal openings did not take place until 1933. After the war the Senior Schools became County Secondary Schools and Quarry Bank children eligible for Grammar School education had to travel to neighbouring towns.

In 1969 the two secondary schools amalgamated and opened on 1 September 1969 as the Secondary Mixed School, under the headship of Mr J.J. Martin. Out of this grew the Thorns School, bringing comprehensive secondary education to Quarry Bank in 1975. Two years later all the pupils found themselves on one site at last in Stockwell Road, and the school grew into the magnificent Thorns Community School that we know today.

More recently another primary school has opened in Quarry Bank – The Thorns Primary School, Thorns Road, completing the scene begun in 1969.

That's not quite the entire story of educational provision in Quarry Bank! If only information was available we could go back to nineteenth-century 'dame schools', one of which is known to have been still dispensing education in the 1890s.

The Arabian Nights. *A school play produced by D'Arcy Jones at Mount Pleasant School about 1937. (Ossie Biddle)*

Quarry Bank's first Board School opened in 1872, two years after School Boards had been established to set about providing universal education. In 1877 the school was greatly expanded so that juniors could be educated in two new single-sex departments, and this building became the province of the mixed infants. (*Ned Williams*)

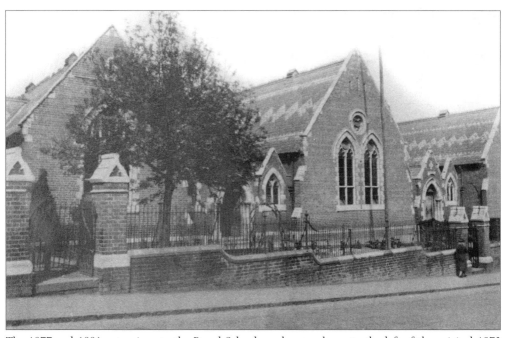

The 1877 and 1881 extensions to the Board School can be seen here, to the left of the original 1872 building seen in the upper picture. Segregated elementary education was provided in these buildings until the 1930s. The replacement can be seen on page 76. (*Frank Webb*)

The Mixed Infants at Quarry Bank School, in 1920. (*Sam Greenaway*)

Later re-organisation led the Infants School to become Quarry Bank First School, but here in the early 1950s it is still t
Infants. Standing, left to right; B.E. Maybury, J. Tipper, T. Madeley. Seated: -?-, J. Butcher, Miss P.M. Prescott (he
mistress 1952–73), Vera Dunn (secretary), Miss Griffiths. (*Vera Dunn*)

In 1925/6 the football team from the boys' department of Quarry Bank School were champions in the Brierley Hill Schools League. The teachers seen here are, left to right; Howard Aston, Albert Tate, Isaac Badger (headmaster), Billy Scriven and Albert Tipper. (*Philip Millward*)

Quarry Bank Boys Junior School staff, early 1950s. Standing, left to right: Howard Aston, Mr Yardley, Mr Green, Mr Scriven, Mr Raybould. Seated: Mrs Rayton, Mr Perry (headmaster), and Ivy Homer (secretary). Messrs Aston and Scriven are also to be seen on the 1925 photograph above. (*Ivy Homer*)

Quarry Bank Infants School, with children preparing a pageant in front of the Junior School building, *c.* 1952. Second from left: Janice Dunn. (*Vera Dunn*)

Quarry Bank Boys Junior School's football team 1950/1 with trophies. Back row, left to right: Brian Cox, Eric Easthope, Colin Dunn, Ivan Clark, Philip Millward. Front row: Brian Thomas, Brian Hickman, Roy Pearson, Ken Genner, Anthony Johnson, Chris Genner, Alan Golding. At the back: Mr Perry is in the centre, and Mr Raybould is on the right. (*Philip Millward*)

From 1932 onwards segregated senior schools were provided at Quarry Bank in Coppice Lane. From 1944 onwards these were called Secondary Schools and the boys' school became known as Conk's College – arising from the headmaster's nickname! This picture of the staff dates from the early 1950s. Standing, left to right: George Smith, Ken Werrett, Ernie Perry, John Tonks, Eric Stanton, A.L. Cox, Basil Hodgkinson. Seated: Bob Roberts, Vera Dunn (secretary), Mr Jeavons (headmaster from 1938 when he took over from Mr Badger), Mrs Brookes (caretaker), and Harry Cox. (*Vera Dunn*)

This picture of the sports field in 1963 is one of the few photographs found that shows the 1932 building provided for the Boys Senior school in Coppice Lane. (*Thorns Community School collection*)

The Girls Secondary School in Coppice Lane, on the opposite side to the boys' school, was on the site now occupied by Coppice Close. In 1951, the girls presented *A Midsummer Night's Dream*, starring Beryl Mountford, Dillis Smith, Barbara Parsons and Margaret Stringer in the main parts, as their contribution to the Festival of Britain celebrations. (*Dillis Baker*)

The cast of a play at the Boys Secondary School line up to take a bow on their school stage in the 1950s. (*Eric Stanton*)

In December 1967 the Secondary Girls School presented a play called *Man Alive* on the stage at the Boys School. Two years later the schools amalgamated. Seated at the front on the right is Sue Hadley, who later became an English teacher at the Thorns School for a time. (*Thorns School collection*)

Phil Millward also had the experience of being both pupil and teacher in Quarry Bank (see page 72). In this picture he appears as a teacher at the Thorns Community School, preparing for a trip to London in the 1980s. The school uniform has changed since then. (*Philip Millward*)

The Quarry Bank County Junior School in Lower High Street, 1970s. When the new senior schools opened in 1932, the schools in Lower High Street (see page 69) became junior boys' and girls' schools. In 1935 work began on erecting this building as a replacement of the nineteenth-century buildings, and pupils were able to move in during April 1937 – the boys on the ground floor, and the girls upstairs. (*John James*)

The Coppice Lane premises of the former Boys Secondary School caught fire in 1974, and can be seen here undergoing demolition. At this stage it was part of the Secondary Mixed school, but later in the year the first classrooms at Stockwell Road came into use, and in September 1975 the school became the Thorns School. (*John James*)

Mount Pleasant Primary School also began life as a Board School, first established in temporary accommodation in the Wesleyan Chapel's Sunday School in 1882, and then in the buildings seen here in 1888. Like its counterpart in Lower High Street, it seems that bigger and better accommodation was required within a few years of opening the school. Unlike the schools in the High Street, Mount Pleasant remained co-educational. Here we see the playground used to celebrate the Queen's Jubilee in 1977. (*John James*)

An aerial view of Mount Pleasant School on 10 September 1988 finds the playground being used to mark the school's centenary. The Infants Department can be seen on the right, and the Junior Mixed Department is on the left, although these had been combined as one school since 1972. (*Gail Bedford*)

When Mount Pleasant School opened on its present site in 1888, the young headmaster was Mr W.E. Hunt – who remained at the helm until 1930. He can be seen on the right of this picture early in his career, with the pupils in Group 4. (*John Shaw*)

Mr Allchurch was headmaster at Mount Pleasant School from 1936 to 1951, and can be seen here with some pupils in 1937 – the year of King George VI's coronation. The pupils include Sally Williams, Cissie Waldron, Arthur Batham, Fred Wellings, Vera Simmons, Mary Hobson, Marian Smith, Irene Scott, Roy Burford and Joseph Jones. (*Vera White*)

Jean James on crossing patrol duty in the early 1980s, and the parents and pupils of Mount Pleasant Primary School cross the road to school for the benefit of the television camera crew seen on the far right. (*John James*)

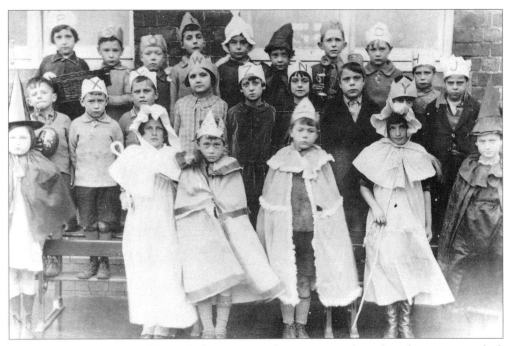

In 1928 the pupils in Miss Widdowson's class at Mount Pleasant are seen dressed to take part in an end-of-term play. Pupils include Jack Randle, Rowland Smith, Eric Walter, Jessie Stevens, Doris Sidaway, Evelyn Hackett, Mary Bennett, Phyllis Bute, Richard Knowles, and Beryl Bloomer — daughter of Christ Church choir master Joe Bloomer. (*Doris Peat/Jessie Yorke*)

A view of Thorns Primary School from the air. This school opened in 1969, and is therefore a relative newcomer! Miss Sturman came as the school's first headmistress from a headship at the Secondary Girls School – combined from that year onwards with the boys' school under Mr Martin's headship. (*Thorns Primary School collection*)

Quarry Bank's Dr Kate Rogers, in her second term of office as Mayor of Dudley, pays a visit to Thorns Primary School in the early 1970s. (*Thorns Primary School collection*)

CHAPTER FIVE

QUARRY BANK AT WORK

The proximity of coal and fireclay to the surface meant that mining and agriculture provided work for the workers of Quarry Bank even before the Industrial Revolution. Industrialisation began with harnessing water power to the business of metal working at Cradley Forge, from which sheets of iron were dragged along the bank of the Stour to a water-driven slitting mill. Strips of iron provided the raw material for nail-making.

Nail-making was not generally a factory based industry – it was a sweated trade that operated as a cottage industry: – folks worked at their hearths at the back of their homes. Chain-making followed the same pattern, although firms like Noah Bloomers did materialise and continued working in the traditional way until recent times. Factory-based work came to the area with the growth of the hollow-ware trade, and a little general engineering, and the products of Quarry Bank were exported world-wide.

A picture taken in the 1970s at Noah Bloomers captures the essence of work at Quarry Bank: The works, and production process, had remained unchanged when the photographer captured this scene. Plentiful supplies of liquid refreshment and an early start still remained characteristics of the chain-maker's day.
(Roy Day)

An early twentieth-century view of the interior of Noah Bloomer's chain works. Noah, assisted by his brothers, founded the firm in 1867 and made great progress based on the quality of his product. By this time the works had about thirty hearths and a proving house, and was making chain for the Admiralty. (*Collection of G. Dunn*)

The scene in Oak Street, outside Noah Bloomer's chain works, just before the First World War in horse-drawn days. Ju... beyond the works, the camera takes in the cemetery and the roof of its little chapel, the houses at the junction of Victor... Road and Coppice Lane, and the wooded hill beyond. (*Collection of John James*)

Chain was often made in the small chain shops at the back of people's homes. Eric Attwood started making chain with his dad, Harry, at the back of the family home in Brick Kiln Street in 1940. This hearth was still in use – probably the last still working on domestic premises – into the 1970s. Eric made chain for over fifty years. (*Eric Attwood*)

Quarry Bank was as well known for hollow-ware production as it was for chain. The galvanised baths in the foreground (riveted together rather than welded as they were later) are a typical hollow-ware product. It is Christmas 1960 and Hilda Mantle's recorder group from Mount Pleasant School has come to play in the works. The men in the background include Don Warwick, whose daughter, Ann, is at the front of the group. (*Doris Peat and Horace Dunn*)

General engineering was also to be found in Quarry Bank. William Hanke started his toolmaking business in a nissen hut in 1919, and is seen here, in the 1960s, talking to Walter Parkinson, chief toolmaker. (*Vicky Horton*)

Gardner-Shaw's bottling plant in the Crown Works, Merry Hill, is seen here in the mid-1950s. Albert Shaw had been producing mineral waters and soft drinks in Quarry Bank since the beginning of the century. (*Bill Bawden*)

The firm of Brettell & Shaw entered the local hollow-ware scene in 1902, as a partnership between T.H. Shaw and W.A. Brettell. Arthur Webb built the Rhodesia Works for the new firm at the top of West Street, and it is here that we can see a household water tank being galvanised in the mid-1950s. (*John Shaw*)

The Rhodesia Works of Brettell & Shaw was extended and altered over the years. This picture was taken in the 'new' bin shop in the late 1950s; Bill Perks and Roy Hunt are bending steel sheets to form Liverpool Corporation bins. The firm supplied a wide variety of bins – most local authorities having their own special design. (*John Shaw*)

This display at a trade show gives only a glimpse of the bewildering variety of galvanised products produced by Brettell & Shaw. By the 1970s the firm also produced bins in plastic, but in the 1900s it had been a mere 'youngster' among older firms well-established in the hollow-ware trade – an industry dominated by Black Country firms. Its progress was based on the quality of its products. (*John Shaw*)

The Brettell & Shaw Rhodesia Works at the top of West Street, late 1950s. The company was bought by Messrs Rhodes & Cartwright in 1980 but is still in business on this site producing both galvanised and plastic products, sometimes using the Bretshaw name. (*John Shaw*)

Clarie Marchant (born 1908) stands by his machine at Ernest Stevens' Judge enamel-ware works in Cradley Heath. Many Quarry Bank folk worked for Ernest Stevens at The Judge. Ernest Stevens (1867–1957) was sole owner of his firm, which he established in the 1890s. From the 1920s onwards he used the fortune he had made as a 'bucket king' to be a public benefactor. In 1925 he established a £10,000 fund to look after the welfare of his workforce. (*Mrs Marchant*)

Ernest Stevens' brother John (1857–1936) established the Jury Hollow-ware company with a works in Thorns Road, and also at Engine Lane in the Lye. John was something of a workaholic and built much of the works himself – later rebuilt by Webbs. This picture of the staff at The Jury was taken in early days; the workforce eventually became very large. (*Mrs S. Raybould*)

Some of the workforce at Jury Holloware in their Home Guard uniforms. Not in uniform, in the centre of the picture, is Henry Silk, and over to the right is Herbert Dunn. Both were managing directors of the public company formed just before John Stevens' death. (*Eric Groves*)

Jury Holloware became a public company in 1935. In the back row, left to right, we can see Herbert Dunn, Henry Silk and Bert Stevens (John's nephew) who were joint managing directors, and in the foreground is Mr Eaton (works manager) and Mr. Chantry – a businessman from Birmingham who joined the Board. They are standing outside the offices at the Jury works. (*Jessie Yorke*)

Whether you employed hundreds, or only employed yourself, Quarry Bank was a small enough community for everyone to be well known. The Thompson family was well known in Quarry Bank, and for years Cecil Thompson repaired boots and shoes from his premises in the High Street. He is seen here in the 1960s. (*John Thompson*)

Cecil's shoe repair shop is seen on the right, while Ann (Nance) Thompson's premises sold soft furnishings from the left-hand side of the building. Now the building is home to Walter Wall – carpet sales. This picture was taken in March 1989. (*Ned Williams*)

Quarry Bank's retail centre – the High Street
and New Street – was a busy place and many
local people worked there. Frank Oliver, a
butcher, is seen here in the doorway of Ernie
Bird's shop in Upper High Street in the 1930s.
(*Arthur Pearson*)

Evelyn Foxall and her brother Jack stand in the doorway of the sweet shop she had taken over at 44 High
Street (previously Marlow's) in the 1930s. Jack ran a dairy farm at Merry Hill and became a local
councillor. (*Frank Webb*)

Quarry Bank eventually boasted four coaching firms (Homer's, Genner's, Hadley's, and Parkes') but such enterprises usually began in quite a modest way. Here is Bert Homer's first Chevrolet charabanc (RF 2850) dating from the mid-1920s. Homer's was bought out by Prospect Coaches (from Lye) in the mid-1970s. (*Geoff Jones*)

A rear view of John Genner's smart 1938 Guy coach (GRE 638) in its dark green and cream livery. The firm's progress into haulage and coaching goes back to the development of John Genner's wet fish business. The wholesale side of this led to making deliveries to other businesses, and haulage was a natural progression. The firm was managed by Mrs Genner and then son Jack. (*Tom and Sybil Genner*)

Robert Chance still delivering milk from a horse-drawn float in the winter of 1969. Robert's father (born 1911) had farmed Freehold Farm in the Caledonia, from which Robert started selling milk locally in 1940. The milk now comes from a dairy as cows no longer graze at Freehold Farm, but Robert still delivers the milk to customers in Quarry Bank; now he uses a van. (*Margaret Priest*)

Every September some Quarry Bankers used to make their way to the hop fields – usually at Cooper's Farm, Knighton-on-Teme. (Fathers – usually chain-makers – stayed in Quarry Bank, but the mothers and children were recruited by a Mrs Stafford and were taken to the farm.) On this occasion, in about 1928, Mrs Glaze, in the centre of the picture, has taken two Quarry Bank ladies, Mrs Davies and Mrs Pearson (on the left) to see hop pickers from Sheffield Street, including Ruth Tipton and Mrs Stevens. (*Ken Tipton*)

CHAPTER SIX

QUARRY BANK LEISURE

Although it might be imagined that Quarry Bankers had too few spare hours and too little money to enjoy their non-working lives, these impediments obviously counted for nothing. If anything, the opposite seems the case and it looks as if Quarry Bankers were busier in their leisure time than in their work!

Most varieties of cultural and sporting activities could be enjoyed in Quarry Bank during the first half of this century. Black Country pastimes such as keeping fowl, racing pigeons, and breeding dogs were all to be found. Many kinds of sporting activities have been pursued: football, cricket, boxing, bowls, tennis, badminton, and so on. Participation in sport was encouraged in local schools, and was well organised among adults. The Stevens Park, church halls, pub bowling greens, and school grounds have all provided facilities.

The cultural life of Quarry Bank is well represented by the choirs, the band, and the drama groups that have all flourished. Every church claims to have had the best choir, and that competition has now been resolved by creating a 'combined choir'. Amateur operatics and dramatics enjoyed an extraordinary existence down at Cradley Forge for many years. Local churches and schools have strong dramatic traditions, and shows are still presented in Quarry Bank at the Thorns Community School. Cinema came to Quarry Bank from 1933 to 1960, and in 1988 a pioneering multiplex cinema was opened less than a mile from the boundary of Quarry Bank!

Add all this to the work of the churches, voluntary organisations, youth organisations, the British Legion and The Old Pals, the Friendly Societies and the political associations, and one wonders how there was ever time to organise the carnivals!

Quarry Bank's Coronet Cinema in Lower High Street decorated for the coronation in 1953. The Coronet was opened on 22 February 1933 by Mr J.E. Dunn – President of the Quarry Bank Hospital Carnival Committee. It belonged to Cecil Cooper and his son-in-law Harold Roberts, and their wives. Mr Roberts ran the cinema for twenty-seven years, closing it on 20 February 1960. (Celia Thorneycroft)

The Quarry Bank Silver Band leads a procession in West Street, with local volunteer firemen immediately behind. Th band began life in 1880 as the Blue Ribbon Temperance Band, founded by Albert and Henry Wootton. Albert's so Walter, the well known photographer, was the band's president for fifty years. In 1970 it became the Dudley Distric Band, and then the Hangers Motors Band. (*Olive Allchurch*)

Carnival Day was an important occasion in Quarry Bank – originally organised to raise funds for local hospitals, and later revamped to support other charities. This 1935 picture gives some impression of the excitement as the procession proceeds down Quarry Bank's decorated High Street. (*Gwen Chapman*)

For an earlier Carnival, the workers from Tubular Holloware, in Oak Street, have formed a jazz band and donned fancy dress to take part in the proceedings. (*Brenda Holloway*)

e carnivals of the early 1950s were held in August, and these carnival queens were photographed by Albert Peat in ens Park. (*Doris Peat*)

The Quarry Bank Festival of Britain Committee who organised a carnival in 1951, including teachers Eric Stanton and D'Arcy Jones, top right, plus Mrs Cooper, Mrs Smith, Mrs Andrews, Eric Lander and Ewart Bloor. The Festival queen is Margaret Castree (attended by Irene Hill). Fairground historians might be puzzled by the identity of the 'Ark' on which they are standing. It is believed to be a machine belonging to Ernie Steel.

Fashions change, and John James photographed these more recent carnival queens – once again in Stevens Park.

In 1971 the Christ Church Young Wives won first prize with their float entered in the Quarry Bank Carnival: The Wives of Henry VIII. Left to right: June Grove, Janet Mason, Margaret Stiff (seen as Carnival queen twenty years earlier on page 96), Janet Parkes, Muriel Fish, Vera White, and with Clara Turner as the axeman. (*June Grove*)

Children's fancy dress competitions were a popular feature of the Quarry Bank carnivals. In this early 1950s picture Albert Peat photographed the children assembled in Stevens Park, looking towards Thorns Road. (*Doris Peat*)

PC Haywood of Quarry Bank helps Pat Phoenix, *Coronation Street*'s Elsie Tanner, make her way through the crowd to open the Quarry Bank Gala. (*Jeanne Haywood*)

Members of the Quarry Bank Operatic Society are seen here taking part in the Gala during August 1972 – using the opportunity to advertise their production of *Oklahoma* presented in the October of that year. (*Vera Dunn*)

The musical and dramatic talents of Quarry Bankers were exploited by a variety of social groups, particularly in the groups that grew up around the churches. This group is taking part in a Sunday School concert before the First World War – presumably in the hall that had recently been rebuilt between Victoria Road and Sheffield Street. (*Marie Billingham*)

Another Sunday School line-up – on this occasion to take part in a concert at Easter 1938. Jack Whitehouse, a lay preacher, is in the centre of the back row, and Mrs McCarthy, the vicar's wife, is second from the right of those standing. On the left is Marie Hanke who married the Revd George Larkin, a later vicar at Christ Church.(*Marie Billingham*)

A Musical Society was established at Cradley Forge Methodist Chapel, and out of this grew the Cradley Forge Operatic & Dramatic Society. From this line up of those taking part at an early Cradley Forge presentation it has been possible to identify Horace Bucknall (second left at the back), Wilf Moore (in the centre), Horace Grove, (who did the lighting), Horace Cartwright, Ezra Harris (musical director) and

The new Sunday School built at Cradley Forge in 1928 (which became the church itself ten years later – see page 52) provided good stage facilities for the Musical Society and the productions became increasingly secular. In the mid-1930s the Society changed its name from Musical Society to Cradley Forge Amateur Operatic & Dramatic Society, and the success of its shows helped pay off the mortgage on the hall. Here is the assembled company of one of the early productions. (*Brenda Holloway*)

The shows at Cradley Forge were particularly successful during the Second World War – playing their part in maintaining morale on the Home Front! The girls lined up in the chorus line for the 1944 production of *Cinderella* put the show on for a week to full houses, and the show had to be repeated. (*Vera Dunn*)

The post-war 1950 Cradley Forge production of *Rio Rita* included dance sequences presented by girls from Celia Cooper's Amblecote-based dancing school. (Celia's father brought the cinema to Quarry Bank.) Celia's girls, left to right, were Ann Hayes, Olive Turner, Helen Coates, Margaret Fincher (in white), Gladys Stokes, Rita Smith, and Nancy Smith. A few years later a new minister on the Methodist Circuit objected to the content of the musical shows and the company had to move elsewhere, before dissolving and eventually being revived as the Quarry Bank Amateur Operatic & Dramatic Society, which has since performed at Netherton Arts Centre. (*Celia Thorneycroft*)

Back to the cast of the 1940 production of *Jack & the Beanstalk*, and in the centre of the back row it is possible to spot Ernie Webb and Dick Bedford. In the centre of the front row is Ivy Bray as Peggy and Jean Smith as Jack. Clarence Tipton and Jack Felton, as Snip and Snop, appear at the back right. (*Vera Dunn*)

Ernie Webb (1907–92) – a leading light of the Cradley Forge productions. Ernie was a good comic improviser and had a strong stage presence. The pantomimes during the early 1940s were usually written and directed by him, but after the war he spent more time with the Cradley Heath Society. He was a builder when off stage, and built his own home in Acres Road. (*Edgar Taylor*)

By the 1960s local shows were being presented by the Show Group, a sub-section of the Young Wives Group at the parish church. Here they are presenting *A Mosey Through Oklahoma*, their first show, at the Church Hall in 1968. The milkmaid is Edwin Gordon – a local painter and decorator with theatrical talents – who was brought in just for this show. (*June Grove*)

The 1970 production put on by the Christ Church Young Wives Show Group was *Songs from the Shows*. Back row, left to right: Brenda Holloway, Freda Foster, Margaret Hill, Florrie Manley, Pat Jones, Addie Harper, Janet Mason. Front row: Betty Wakeman, Margaret Newton, Muriel Fish, Audrey Davies, Trudy Castree, June Grove. (*June Grove*)

The First Quarry Bank Scout Troop was authorised in 1922 and met at the the Church Hall, Victoria Road. By 1928 Harry Hawkeswood, of the local family who ran the ironmongery business at the top of the High Street, was scout master. He is seen here in the centre of the back row of this picture showing Cubs, Scouts and Rover Scouts. (*Jean Malik*)

In the 1970s the Scouts became Sea Scouts, and from 1980 onwards met at their new headquarters in Bobs Coppice Walk. In this picture, taken on 3 April 1982, Eric Lander, President of the Old Scouts, presents a new standard to the troop. (Eric was last seen on page 96 about thirty years earlier!) (*Jack Beddall*)

In 1981 the Sea Scouts of Quarry Bank and Lye amalgamated. Jack Beddall of the Quarry Bank Old Scout & Friends Association greets Margaret Perks, chair of the combined Quarry Bank & Lye 1st Sea Scouts at the Bobs Coppice HQ. (*Jack Beddall*)

Quarry Bank lads go camping at Coven in 1951. Eric Stanton, a teacher at Quarry Bank Secondary Boys School (on the right) takes a group to camp that includes Jones, Beddard, Hayne, Worton, Marchant, Genner, Griffiths and Porter. (*Eric Stanton*)

Kate Rogers started a successful Darby & Joan Club at the Quarry Bank Community Centre, and here in the mid-1970s, three ladies who have entered the Easter Bonnet competition have a word with the vicar, the Revd Tom Chapman. Lilian Attwood is in the centre of the threesome.(*Lillian Attwood*)

The Quarry Banker's love of dressing up knows no bounds. A 1980s scene in the Community Centre reveals a group of revellers about to trawl the local pubs while fund-raising for the Quarry Bank Middle School annual fête – organised by Maureen Phillips. (*Minnie Taylor*)

Quarry Bank Conservative Club, *c.* 1918. Arthur Webb, the builder, dominates the back row in his top hat. (The gentleman on the left of the middle row – also wearing a top hat – was the local undertaker.) Frank Webb (Arthur's brother) sits in the centre in the uniform of the Staffordshire Yeomanry. Hatless in the front row are the young men of Quarry Bank: second from left is Simeon Wood, and third from left is John Genner, both of whom will later change their political allegiance. (*Frank Webb*)

Arthur Webb, in his capacity as a builder, rebuilt the building in the Upper High Street that became the Conservative Club, which is being formally opened in this picture of about 1910. Frank Webb (Arthur Webb's son) stands just behind the fence in a cap. His father and uncle are also in the scene. The opening is being conducted by Sir Arthur Buscoyne – MP for Dudley. (*Frank Webb*)

The Quarry Bank Labour Club stands at the opposite (lower) end of the High Street, with the Liberals in between the two! The roof of the old New Street Chapel can be seen in the background. The Labour Club was started about 1918 by young and disaffected members of the Liberal Club, and first met in a private house in New Street. This building is on the site of the former bowling green, behind premises on the High Street. (*Dave Whyley*)

The Labour Party made good electoral progress in Quarry Bank at Urban District Council level and then at Staffordshire County Council level. John Henry Stringer was the first Labour County Councillor to be elected from Quarry Bank – in the March 1925 election. (*Arthur Pearson*)

Quarry Bank Celtic Football Club was started during the Second World War and its original team is seen here, in their blue strip with white collars, in 1946. Back row, left to right: Billy Amplett, Bob Checketts, Charles Cooper, Cedric Evans, Bernard Stevens, Zak Bloomer, Cyril Cartwright (manager). Middle row: Reg Waldron, Reg Jasper, Freddie Knight, Noah Allen, Tom Cartwright. Front row: Verne Clements and Colin Connop. (*Charles Cooper*)

unns Bank Football Club, March 1976. Back row, left to right: B. Turner, G. Westwood, T. Watts, T. Dingley, Dimmock, S. Sidaway, D. Brooks, G. Clews, D. Penn, and J. Cartwright. Front row: J. Biddle, B. Undrill, D. Able, Nock (captain), M. Morgan, C. Penn, M. Solitan. Seated: J. Dingley. (*Bessie Cranton*)

Just as the schools and Sunday Schools promoted musical and dramatic activity, they also promoted interest in sports. In its day, the Mount Pleasant Old Boys was a formidable team — trained by Harry Oliver every Monday evening. (*John Robinson*)

The Cradley Forge Sunday School also produced a successful football team — seen here posing as League Champions in 1937. Back row, left to right: Jack Williams, Jack Homer, William Allport, ? Dunn, George Davis, Howard North, Frank Davis. Middle row: Reg Adams, Sidney Priest, Edgar Taylor (captain), Albert Batham, Bert Jeavons. Front row: Jimmy Green, Reg Johnson, Tom Batham. (*Edgar Taylor*)

The Quarry Bank Tennis Club, of Edwardian times, found space for a court and a pavilion out on the rural fringe of Quarry Bank by Coppice Lane. This well-dressed group includes a few familiar faces – such as Arthur Webb, second from the right in the back row. In more recent times the club has become established on ground by Two Woods Lane. (*Frank Webb*)

The Sunday School building in Victoria Street has been large enough to provide a home to many different activities, from jumble sales to concerts, from drama to sporting activities. Two Worcestershire schoolboys badminton champs emerged from the Quarry Bank Church Badminton Club in 1974: Michael Grove and Richard Mason. (*June Grove*)

At one time many local public houses found space for a bowling green. One of these survives at The White Horse in New Street, and it is here that we find members of the bowling club, plus two dogs, posing for a photograph in about 1928. Left to right: Albert Cooper, Mr. Capewell, Fred Gale, Mr Williams, George Tristram, Major Hickman, Bill Grazier, Sam Clarke and Harry Willetts. (*J. and M. Watton*)

Another bowling club was attached to the Labour Club. They are seen here at the green at the back of the club just after the war, with a trophy won in the Sidaway League, which they had won for the fifth time in 1945. Front row, left to right: George Palmer, Councillor Simeon Wood, Albert Tipton, Arthur Henderson MP, Joe Round (captain), Joe Goodwin, Jack Genner, Charles Cooper and Councillor Sid Whitehouse. (Messrs Wood and Genner were last seen among the Conservatives on page 107.) Players at the back include Charley Dimmock, Harry Ball and Billy Smith, but others have not been identified. (*Tom and Sybil Genner*)

In 1940 a Kennel Club Breeders Diploma was awarded to Jack Dunn, of Quarry Bank, as breeder of the champion dog 'Gentleman Jim'. As 'Jim' was unable to sign his own photograph, the next best thing was to have the card to Jack signed by Joe Mallen, distinguished local chain-maker and expert dog-breeder who met regularly with his fellow-breeders at the Old Cross Guns in Cradley Heath. (*Horace Dunn*)

Jack Dunn's dog had two puppies, and the one that he gave to his son Horace grew up to be another champion Staffordshire Bull Terrier: 'Thornhill Pride'. Here is Horace with the new champion just after the war. (*Horace Dunn*)

Most chain-making communities established a reputation for using their leisure time to breed dogs, fowl and pigeons, and using their athletic skills in pursuits like prize-fighting. Harry Attwood was a well-known local boxer, who would join Barney Tooley of Brierley Hill in taking part in fights in the boxing booths that travelled with the local fairs. (*Horace Dunn*)

George Dunn also came from the chain-making community of Quarry Bank and is seen here, in 1906, as the winner of the Sunday Schools Athletics Trophy. George Dunn (1887 – 1975) is best remembered as 'The Minstrel of Quarry Bank'. Between the wars he had been well known as a singer and story-teller in local pubs and at private parties. His memory stretched back to Victoria's Jubilee and beyond, and he was able to describe what it was like to start work at Noah Bloomer's in 1903, and then at the 'Judge'. His talents and rich store of memories were rediscovered in 1971, his songs and stories were collected, he recorded an LP, and his biography was written! (*H. Proctor*)

CHAPTER SEVEN

PEOPLE & EVENTS

Quarry Bank has been small enough to enjoy a village-like sense of community. The names of key families appear over and over again and faces reappear in a variety of contexts in the photographs throughout this book. Often an individual played a number of roles in the life of the local community – in business and industry, in church or chapel, in the political clubs and friendly societies, on the council, on the magistrates bench, hospital committees, carnival committees, plus a range of sports and social activities.

In some cases representatives of these families are still to be found in Quarry Bank. In other cases they have moved westwards to Stourbridge or Kingswinford in search of cleaner air. No doubt some ex-Quarry Bankers now live on the other side of the world. Faced with the fact that many of the families who built Quarry Bank are now dispersed, and that the local population consists of large numbers of newcomers bewildered by these names, the time has come for Quarry Bankers to sit down and invent a new sense of community.

Almost any excuse provided an opportunity for Quarry Bankers to come together socially as many of the photographs testify. One committee that turned out to be a comprehensive 'Who's Who' of Quarry Bank of the time was the group assembled to prepare local events to celebrate the coronation of King George V in 1911. They were photographed in the garden of Mount Pleasant House, now the home of Frank Webb. Back row, left to right: S. Yardley, W.E. Hunt, Frank Webb, Joe Goodwin, Albert Shaw, F. Hawkeswood, Mr Proctor, Mr Turner, H. Thorneycroft, -?-. Middle row: the wives of the above. Front row: the Revd Mr Morris, H. Dunn, possibly Simeon Wood and four men so far unidentified. (Gladys Davies)

Here we find the Webb family at the back of their home at 51 High Street Quarry Bank, *c.* 1910; Mervyn, Mrs Clara Maria Webb (née Hazlehurst), Frank, Mr Arthur Webb, whose building firm built so much of Quarry Bank, and Aunt Lizzie (Mrs Webb's sister). (*Frank Webb*)

The Shaw family – thought to be photographed at the back of 'Lamsdale', the house built for the family by Arthur Webb, in Thorns Road – looking out over fields! Thomas Hingley Shaw Snr and his wife are top left; T.H. Shaw Jnr is in the centre of the front row, and Lizzie Shaw, the oldest child, is on the right. The former married May Hunt, the daughter of Mount Pleasant School's headmaster, and the latter became headmistress at Enville Road. School, Stourbridge. The Shaws are associated with the local hollow-ware firm Brettell & Shaw (see pages 85–6). (*John Shaw*)

Ernest Stevens (1867–1957) and his wife Mary (1870–1925) – well-known public figures in Quarry Bank, Stourbridge and the Lye. Edward Stevens had three sons and a daughter: John, William, Ernest and Lucy. John and William financed Ernest's education at Stourbridge Grammar School, to which he walked every day from Quarry Bank. The family business was established in Brickkiln Street and eventually Ernest took this over and rebuilt the company on his own – moving it to Cradley Heath. This was the famous 'Judge' hollow-ware firm. William and John countered this with the 'Jury' hollow-ware firm, with premises in Thorns Road.

Ernest's great success as a businessman gave him the means to become a public benefactor – possibly influenced by his wife. Mary came from the Amblecote Road and was a member of the Wesleyan congregation at Mount Pleasant. For the first ten years of their married life they lived at the Sycamores in Thorns Road.

During the First World War Mary was very active in local public work in Quarry Bank and Stourbridge, to which they had moved. After the war the Stevens began making generous gifts to the communities of which they were a part, but as this gained momentum Mary died. From the summer of 1925 onwards the gifts continued, but from then on as gifts from Ernest in memory of his wife. The part that Quarry Bank played in the lives of the Stevens and, in turn, the part their lives played in the communities of the south-western corner of the Black Country, are matters that have yet to be fully explored and understood. (*From portraits supplied by Jessie Yorke*)

David Poole was once apprenticed to Arthur
Webb as a carpenter but found another career as
a ventriloquist. The picture dates from the first
decade of this century. Although never a major
star, David enjoyed a very long career on the
variety stage. (In one local theatre his first
appearance was in 1903, his last was in 1947!)
The chap on the left was 'Johnny Green'.
(*Frank Webb*)

John Genner, wet fish retailer and wholesaler of
Quarry Bank, appears in several pictures in this
collection. He claimed to be the only Quarry
Banker to have to wear a kilt – as a result of
joining a Scottish regiment during the First World
War! (*Tom and Sybil Genner*)

Percy Beddall and his daughter Elsie appearing as 'Elmar & Elsie', the well-known equilibrists. Percy was born in Quarry Bank but travelled to Australia and South Africa while on his journey into show business. He returned to Church Street, Quarry Bank, in about 1920 with his wife Stella and daughter Elsie, and they then toured the British variety theatres until Elsie's 'retirement' in 1932. This was brought about by Elsie's marriage to Jack Genner, who looked after the Genner transport business. (*via Stan Hill*)

Major Cranton of Dunns Bank was a keen horticulturalist, and arranged the horticultural shows in Quarry Bank. In 1967 he was one of the founders of the West Midlands Rose Society and organised the first annual show for the society at Claverley in that year. (*Bessie Cranton*)

Frank Webb, the younger son of Arthur Webb, married Ida Roberts at Christ Church in 1930. Ida came from the family of corn-millers at the far end of Mount Pleasant and attended the Wesleyan Chapel where the reception was held. (The picture was taken at the back of her family's house.) The best man was Harry Hawkeswood, from the family associated with the ironmongery shop – he can be seen in his capacity as scoutmaster on page 104. (*Frank Webb*)

Thomas Davies and Ivy Cartwright also married at Christ Church – on 16 March 1940 – and their wedding picture was taken outside 58 Saltwells Road, one of the houses of Quarry Bank's 'White City'. The white rendering is quite clearly visible in the picture. (*Roy Smith*)

The 'White City' mentioned on the opposite page is seen here in one of Kendall's 1930s postcard views of Quarry Bank. The entrance to the 'White City' from Coppice Lane also reveals the original whiteness of these Council houses erected just after the First World War. At one time the road through the estate became White City Road, and then reverted to Saltwells Road. Confusion with Netherton's road of the same name, not far away, has led to it being called White City Road again – but the houses are no longer white! (*Judith Simpson*)

The new brick walls of the houses in the 'White City' can be seen clearly as we return to the front door of no. 58, last seen on the opposite page in 1940! Lisa Smith stands by the front door dressed for a competition – judged by Dr Fair – organised for the Jubilee Celebrations on 7 June 1977. (*Roy Smith*)

Private Arthur Taylor of 10 West Street was one of Quarry Bank's best-known First World War heroes as a result of hi
widely publicised return home on 23 August 1915. Arthur was a regular soldier in the 2nd Battalion Worceste
Regiment, but had previously worked for Brettell & Shaw. The firm arranged his collection from Dudley Port statio
when he was granted a few days' leave from treatment in a war hospital. Bower Lane and West Street were adorned i
flags for his reunion with his wife and eight-month-old baby, with whom he stands in this picture. (*E. Cox*)

Private Taylor's view of Bower Lane, by Mrs Cartwright's toffee shop, looking towards the Gate Hangs Well public ho
as he returned briefly to Quarry Bank. The extent of his wounds and the X-ray he carried showing the bullet lodged i
abdomen shocked local residents. He returned to his regiment after this visit and was killed later in the war. (*Clifford Sh*

Special events celebrated in Quarry Bank have ranged from moments in national history to obscure incidents in very localised history. In this picture, customers at the Saltwells Inn have arranged a children's party to mark the coronation of King George VI in 1937. (*Brenda Holloway*)

A much more local event took place to mark the opening of the new toilets at the Church Tavern in June 1962. This was organised by landlord Ken Shepherd (right) who had previously been stage manager at the Dudley Hippodrome. He used his show-biz connections to invite Alan French to play Miss Quarry Bank and Loretta to pose on the engine. (*The late Ken Shepherd's collection*)

The firm's annual outing always provided a good moment for a memorable photograph. At the end of the 1920s Brettell & Shaw hired this Guy 'chara' from Tours & Transport of Wolverhampton for the works trip. T.H. Shaw Jnr sits near the front by Miss Price, his secretary, and Mrs M.E. Shaw. Behind them is Mr Victor Brettell and his wife, and at the back are John Warwick and works foreman Ben Taylor. (*John Shaw*)

Coaches line up outside the Conservative Club in Upper High Street for a members' outing on a showery day in the early 1950s. It is just possible to catch a glimpse of the front of the Conservative Club building (Excelsior House, of 1894) which is now obscured by a shallow brick extension. (*Jack Beddall*)

Of the many occasions when Quarry Bankers came together with a great sense of social purpose, the parades and carnivals must be the strongest manifestations of community spirit. The Coronation Committee of 1911 (page 115) worked hard to provide two days of activity of which Quarry Bank could be proud, at a time when the Urban District Council was feeling the pinch. Another view of the parade seen on page 8 shows the Staffordshire Yeomanry in the procession down the High Street. (*I.A. Homer*)

Sunday School Parades also brought crowds to the streets. PC Bobby Clark escorts the procession up the High Street past the Church Tavern in about 1913. (*Mary Hill*)

A reminder of how quickly the face of Quarry Bank can change comes in the form of this view of the crossroads at the centre of the township. Beyond the Blue Ball we can see that Thorns Avenue continued directly to the crossroads in the 1970s and traffic congestion is quite mild (see page 9). (*John James*)

As we started this book in the autumn of 1997, destruction of property on all sides of this crossroads was gaining momentum. In January 1998 major work began on re-modelling this congested junction and the stretch of Merry Hill leading down to the Coppice Lane Island (see page 27). Behind the Blue Ball a new highway has been pushed across Sun Street to join the High Street opposite the top of Park Road – as seen in this picture of 1 May 1998. By the end of 1998 the face of Quarry Bank will have changed again. (*Ned Williams*)

ACKNOWLEDGEMENTS

The Local History Group at Mount Pleasant Primary School has included the following people, to which we have added the names of the many people who have handed in photographs to members of the group. Further names have been added to acknowledge others who have helped without necessarily providing photographs or attending the group, but have added to the sum total of this book. Apologies to those left out: we have received so much help, it has often been difficult to keep track of everyone involved.

Olive Allchurch, Ivy Astley, Eric Attwood, Lilian Attwood, D. Baker, Bill Bawden, Jack Beddall, Julie Bird, Mary Brookes, Oswald Biddle, Marie Billingham, Doreen Cartwright, Gwen Chapman, the Rev. Tom Chapman, Robert Chell, Charles Cooper, E. Cox, Bessie Cranton, Gladys Davies, J. Davies, Roy Day, Bram and Vera Dunn, Jabe Edwards, Horace Dunn, Jane Geddes, Tom and Sybil Genner, Jack Genner, S. Greenaway, Eric Grove, June Grove, Emma and Ron Hanglin, Jeanne Haywood, Mary Hill, Stan Hill, Brenda Holloway, Walter Hughes, Ivy Homer, Vicky Horton, John James, Geoff Jones, Hilda and Joyce Mantle, Nancy Marchant, Janet Mason, Patricia Mattocks, Sister Janice Mills, Philip Millward, Joan and Arthur Pearson, Doris Peat, Phyllis Prescott, Margaret Priest, S. Raybould, Charmayne Redding, Ken Rock, John Robinson, Pauline Rollason, Mary Rousell, Clifford Shaw, John Shaw, Judith Simpson, Pat and Sylvia Shaw, Roy Smith, Eric Stanton, Alan Southall, Edgar Taylor, Minnie Taylor, John Thompson, Celia Thorneycroft, Ken Tipton, M. Watson, John and Margaret Watton, Frank Webb, Frank Whiley, Dave Whyley, Joy Woodhouse, Gemma Wright, Jessie Yorke.

And thanks to Mount Pleasant School, Quarry Bank School, Thorns Primary School and Thorns Community School, plus library staff at Brierley Hill, Stourbridge, and Mount Pleasant, Coseley. Thanks to Jan Endean in Wolverhampton for endless black and white photograph copying.

Each photograph has been credited but the name given refers to the source of the print we have used. This is not necessarily the name of the photographer. Every effort has been made to ascertain the copyright of the photographs used but in some cases this remains obscure. The principal postcard photographers of Quarry Bank have been Walter Wootton, E. Beech, John Price, and the Kendall Series, and this has been made clear in the captions. John James and Dave Whyley have made a topographical photographic record of Quarry Bank in recent times, but such is the speed of change that their work also qualifies as 'old photographs'.

An early picture of the Quarry Bank town band, whose history is briefly outlined on page 94. (*Olive Allchurch*)